The Temple on Monday

The Temple on Monday

by

Tom Crawford

EWU
P·R·E·S·S

Eastern Washington University Press
Spokane, Washington

Cover design by Scott Poole
Book design by Joelean Copeland

Library in Congress Catatloging-in-Publication Data

Crawford, Tom, 1939—
       The temple on monday/ by Tom Crawford
              p. cm.
ISBN 0-910055-72-6 (pbk.)
       I. Title

PS3553.r296 T4 2001
811'.54—dc21

                              00-067742

for yd

Table of Contents

SECTION I

SECTION II

SECTION III

SECTION IV

We're talking of hope here, hope & dreams, not of disease & cure.

— Sandra Loy, from *Police Notebooks*

Buddha's cleared out
and left no incense burning.
Besides you there's nothing in the temple
now to hang your hat on.
The quiet is the quiet of snow,
the bell, immense, silent.
Only a few good words the monks left behind lying
around
on the floor
and a worn pillow—that's it
and the light, stoop shouldered,
coming through a low door.

I

Slow Going

My only speed is to look around.
So naturally I go slow considering the leaves
because look how long it took them
before they could let go, each one
deciding for itself the way down.

On city streets I make very little headway.
Walking gets me past a building
so slowly I'm usually in the way
and if friends are with me
they begin to think up places
where we can meet later.

It's OK. I love them for allowing me
my slowness. In Korea where I live now
there are strict laws against not moving fast
which means besides living in the wrong country
bus doors open and close
sometimes before I can get on or off.
Then heads turn the whole length of the bus
to watch me on the curb being left behind.

When kids wave I wave back

or if I'm inside and can't get off
I usually take it as a sign I have further to go.

My German grandmother used to tell me
all the time, "Tommy, take your time,"
which is what I thought the lovely autumn poster in
the elevator

in downtown Kwangju was saying the other day—
red leaves
big as your hand floating in a little creek
beside a Buddhist temple.
It took me half an hour of riding up and down
to get my fill, all the time
being pushed around by businessmen.

I can't think of anything fast that's good
if the eye can't rest there.

My love has a place I call home
or sometimes the moon rising.
We laugh about that,
my need to always name what I feel around me.

Any ritual to clear the mind.
I brush my teeth. Wear loose clothes. Stay quiet.
Temples are a distraction—too beautiful
unless it's Monday in Korea and raining.
The older the better—what's broken, gray,
the stupas cocked sideways and beaten down,
monument to lichen, decay, qualifies.
Best of all, though, memory, the hand
involuntarily making its way
toward the mouth,
the bent face, for what we imagine lost.

Lanterns tied to the branches of trees
line the road
where they sway like gorgeous birds,
the orange glow each official prayer gives off
on Buddha's birthday,
the practical side to faith—month
for new tiles, or to pay the electric bill
of the thousand-lighted Bodhisattva.

We've come so late all the monks are in bed.
Only the pu koo bird is still up
sailing its ancient song like a white ball
over the roof of the temple.

In America, in Flint, Michigan, 45 years ago,
on my 9th birthday, Buddha was a red bicycle
I could get ahold of—chrome handle bars,

black, leather seat,
kickstand,
red reflectors
and me riding it full speed,
no chain guard
through Kearsley Park Cemetery
at night.

Autumn

Trees.
Like them I am learning to be
in whatever color I can manage
by just standing still.

There is nowhere in the world
right now that is not autumn.

The sun is democratic
and turns us all around
to love the ends of things
as much as their beginnings.

To make a quiet stand
for the down-falling leaves
which only means to watch them grow
into their best expression
and leave us, finally, in a gust of wind,

warmed and speechless.

Stating the Problem

We love the morning
because, well, we don't know why
something got up with us
kinder than we are
and quieter
and the tears springing
into our eyes
over an ordinary sunrise
startle us.

So, why are we already turning
away, looking for our clothes,
wanting the sadness
of the morning paper?

There was a bright bud
opening inside
for a moment, wasn't there?

What happened then
that we could not stand it,
that we are such lousy gardeners?

Fish

Outside it's Korea and snowing.
White flakes float in under the eaves
and slide sideways into my window.
Inside I'm talking to this big Asian ink brush
about a fish I'd like us to draw.
I've loaded it with the blackest ink
and now I'm holding it, poised
over a clean sheet of 3-foot-long white paper.
I'm keeping my voice down
though I'm pretty excited
and the snow falling outside doesn't help,
but here's what I say, "You know
already from the way I'm holding you
that I'm not an artist."
All right, that's out in the open.
It can't hurt, I figure, to own up
to what the brush knows anyway.
"I'm asking for just one terrible black fish," I say
and inch the brush closer to the white paper.
I know it's cheap of me
to imagine the brush could actually be tempted this way.
Outside snow's beginning to pile up
on the metal railing, the patio.
The bare branches of the maple below my apartment
look like tall zebras. Very beautiful.
In the distance the buildings of Kwangju
grow even bigger, darker, in the falling snow.
"This fish, I only want to look at it!" I implore.
"If not the whole fish, then at least some part of it.
Draw me an eye for god-sakes!"
I hate it when my voice gives me away

like some old man who's discovered
he's on the wrong bus.
In my hand is a long length of yellow bamboo with a
shock of horse hair black with ink.
Made in Korea, it says,
and not the Romantic Period. I let that go.
There will always be the detractors.
Outside it's growing dark, Presbyterian
as the red, neon crosses begin to come on
across the city.
I put my tongue on the glass window
to feel the cold,
to feel what snow feels.
If I could leave my body right now
where would I go more amazing than this—
this black fish for company,
alive down there somewhere in the paper
and me, up here,
happy, alone in the snow.

Below my director's chair
I can just make out the shape of my white toes
in the dark. Outside,
the first thin wash of blue light
spreads west over the city.
No human voice out there
to call the Moslems to prayer.
Only the growing hiss and grind
of black tires on wet asphalt—the Barks
chasing the Kims down wet streets
in the half dark, shooting for their best time.
Someone in the Samsung Plaza hits the switch,
always around 6:00, and the tallest building in
Kwangju
goes black, ahead of 100 or more
Presbyterian red neon crosses arguing
last, I suppose, is first
I wiggle my toes to be sure
that at the other end of me
everything still works. They do.
In this light, now a little bluer, up here
my life suddenly seems manageable,
as if just getting up deserved some kind of applause.
It's where I seem to fit in, in this life,
that quiet half hour between darkness and daylight.

Mr. Overstreet's Shoes

...For Mr. Overstreet from Georgia, who left Kwangju in
1992 after his students burned the American flag.

You were big. Probably a meat & potatoes man to
look at the way the soles sunk under your great
weight, Mr. Overstreet. These old Florsheims and sad
rumor are all you left behind to prove you once
taught here. The worn, black leather, if one listens,
says you were solitary, heavy on your feet, and
probably an idealist. Maybe it's just the big, Fall
moon and what these size 12s point toward on the
Korean Peninsula that drive this poem: the mounds
of dirt—ancestral tombs on the slope of the hill next
to the library, long forgotten and melting like pale,
green soap, back into the landscape you walked by
everyday. The beautiful students, especially the young
women with thick, black hair and perfect teeth who,
when they smile, are taught to cover their mouths
with their hands. Everything we do hides something.
Your feet were ugly. Board-flat arches. Hunchback
insteps that twisted the tongues sideways. You can
see my interest is mostly in wear and tear. These
almost interchangeable lives. You've seen them too, in
the villages here, the old women out beating their
colored clothes on the same worn stones. With their
ancient knuckles they push the suds through the red
shirts, the black socks, over and over until after a
while the water comes clean.

Patriots

Aren't we the true patriots,
up all night, undressing for our countries?
Isn't this what the old war was really about,
blurring the distinction between tongues
where Korean kisses slowly move
the dollar up
against the soft won?
Who wants to fight anyway
with no shoes on,
eating out of the same ceramic bowls
(fall geese flying through blue glaze),
and us feeling friendly
and already so close to the floor.
The old Taoist
in the painting behind us
climbing up Fishhead Mountain
would approve of our position,
we think, to give in. That is why
we have tied our clothes together,
your dress around my pants,
in case worse comes to worst,
the flag we plan to wave.

Star

At night, late, and when it's quiet
in the house
sometimes a small blue star appears
in my window.
Now I have begun to look for it
and lie very still on the floor
in the dark
to watch it slowly move over me
sometimes disappearing
behind low clouds
then suddenly reappearing again.
Now I'm thinking of giving it a name,
my star,
even though I know it will not stay long
and then I begin to feel a great distance
out there
my words cannot reach
and I think this is my life also
to be alone, finally,
and to love the world in passing.

Valentine's Candy

It's one of those nights
stumbling around my room
drunk on blue
over the roof of the house
so dark inside the heart
shaped box of chocolates
I cry
just to lift one out
in its own crisp wrapper.

We love the stars don't we?
The dimly lit room, solitude.
What can I do now
but put it in my mouth
though the teeth are no match
for the brown caramel,
for the liquor of so much sky.

Ancestral Worship

Today I have nothing
better to do than watch the Korean snow
gather in the bare arms of the maple
below my apartment window.
"Life is long," I'm fond of saying
and long enough
for me to recall all those
I did not love enough—
my uncle, the half of him I remember
sticking out from under his Buick
or Ford in gray coveralls and black oily shoes,
pushing himself along on his creeper
and his gentle voice, "Tom, get me
a 3/8 open-end and the WD."
He's dead. And by now a hundred other
ghosts of the heart—
the people who got me here.
Here where we are still alive
(let's not define it), the white Buddha
covering everything, says, quietly,
shut up.
I try to imagine the end, anyway,
obviously an American death,
a blue car, vintage, pulling up to the curb—
what waves snow to stop?
And what's left to miss? Given a chance to answer
I might say, the chrome 1/2 inch socket,
short extension.

In the House of Snow

This is our fate
to have to take our seats again
to be overruled by snow.

In here quiet settles everything.
All of our noisy objections
come back white.

Is there a god or isn't there?

We no longer ask

the snow piling up
against the dark buildings,
bare trees

the old woman
trudging through it
carrying her armload of firewood.

Soul

The soul, I imagine, lifts up out of the body through
the top of the head when a person dies. But I
suppose it could come out about anywhere and it
would be refreshing if, for once, it were to come out
in color, or better yet, carrying a flag. Something to
show us it really was on its way. The flag wouldn't
have to be large, or American, the kind you see on
car lots in Los Angeles, as big as a god-damn house.
But something pretty we could follow with our eyes
up toward the ceiling. Or if the person died outside,
maybe a wave of blue light ascending through the
branches of a tree. That's the problem with death,
isn't it, that it doesn't meet our expectations in life?
To be focused on the problem seems to be the
problem. We want a send-off that we can recognize,
the way a white cruise ship might pull very gradually
away from the dock, the stretch of water widening
between the steel hull and the wooden piles, confetti
streaming from the handrails, people smiling, crying,
waving handkerchiefs. It's cheap, isn't it, to want the
ordinary? That I can't envision something greater
than I can envision really pisses me off. You can see
that I'm not arguing for the existence of the soul,
that is to say, I'm a man of faith, but why shouldn't
we have a glimpse of it floating away? And I say
floating because in death I can't imagine us still
running before the bank closes. In violent death, I've
read, the soul literally jumps out of the body and
somersaults like a gymnast across the floor. I don't

know about that but the image is beautiful. The other night in Korea—it was very late actually and I had the lights off so I could sit by the window and watch the stars—a strange feeling came over me. I wasn't sick. But it was as if something inside of me was getting up for the first time in my 55 years and moving. It wasn't in a hurry either. More the way a bear moves, deliberately and with authority.

Morning Light

Morning comes gradual
over Mudong mountain
like crawling
over a high fence
in a pair of blue pants
one leg at a time.
It's as if light had an appointment
to keep with what's ordinary—
the stubbled rice fields,
bare winter trees
or the gray farm house
where the very old live
who can't sleep anymore
so lean in their doorway
to watch the world
become
gradually familiar.
Then the rooster's crow
soothes like warm rice gruel
and getting around
again
seems worthwhile.

II

Stones

In the beginning
the stones are put in the crib
by the grandmother, the mother
the big sister. This is an old tradition.
The baby girl is encouraged to pick them up
everyday, in order to grow stronger.

After only a few weeks the stones are replaced
by heavier ones
which she is again urged to lift.
At no time is the mother cruel
about the stones. She loves her daughter
but she does insist that the baby lift them.
She does this by singing to her the history of stones
and how women along the Korean Peninsula
have always carried them.

When the daughter begins to wear clothes
the stones, even heavier ones now, are loaded
into her small pockets. Walking is not easy
with so many stones to carry
but her mother is pleased
when her daughter begins to adjust
to the weight of them. She loves her parents
and besides, by now she's grown accustomed
to the fatigue of being born a girl.

This is her fate, they tell her, to be tired.
She, of course, believes it
because she cannot remember a time
when she did not carry stones.

So, it's a happy time,
the moment her parents have been waiting for,
their daughter coming into womanhood—
the full weight of it.

When you look into a Korean woman's eyes
you want to stare
at something far back,
dark,
older even than the whole, sad Peninsula.

Trees

...for David Duncan in America

"And he looked up and said, 'I see men as trees, walking.'"

I.

We were told to be good
and not to hurt anybody
which was not unreasonable.
My friend at the airport in Spokane
must have felt this when he began to tremble
and then wonder why
everyone else wasn't crying
for Christ-sakes.

Inside the tree there is an engine
so finely tuned we don't hear it
anymore just walking by
or even when we bend down
among the leaves to tie our shoes.
We don't know the danger we're in,
that we plan, everyday now, to be run over
by our own deafness.

Only autumn can jar our stony instincts
into song, enough to get us
all out the back door
and standing, arm over each others' shoulders
and leaning into brother, sister, friend,
smiling mothers and grave fathers

forever in front of the red maple
for the group shot.

2.

In a famous black and white photograph
the man in front is wearing a bird mask,
the Raven,
with feathered arms held out
flapping them like wings.
The other men are all leaning forward
in their seats, pushing wooden paddles
into the water along side the dugout.
Their shoulders are bare, wet,
shining against the gunnel
in white spray.
They're moving right along.

3.

When lift overtakes drag
the pilot knows he is still on the earth
but it is OK now to bring up
the nose of the plane
so that we might not all perish.
And because he is not a holy man
we squeeze the arm rest,
remind ourselves that flying
afterall, is safer than driving.
Only the faithful among us
are able to watch out the window
calmly, the silver wing lift
gracefully up
over the long line
of black oaks along the river.

Tea Bowl

...for Len Hudson

My friend's tea bowl, a lumpy brown thing, more
toad than vessel, and which he made with his own
hands, and handed to me the other day in America.
"Take it back to Korea." He knew that I was fond of
that piece...I suppose because I would unconsciously
take it off the shelf and cradled in my hands, carry it
around exploring its lovely imperfections, watching
the light play on the dark glaze. Sometimes it would
start a conversation between us, again, about beauty.
Longing. In Yong Bong-dong, Kwangju, South Korea,
at the corner of my apartment building and in the
drain system under a heavy steel cover lives a big
toad, or maybe it's a frog. It doesn't really matter. But
sometimes at night, and only when it's cool or
raining, it begins to croak. If I'm lucky enough to be
walking by when it starts up, I stop to listen. This is
a busy place with people coming and going along a
narrow path leading to the south college gate. When
I stop like that, suddenly, and peer down at the steel
drain cover, I create a sort of traffic jam. People have
to adjust their stride in order to get around me. And
often they are curious or confused about my
behavior. It's less that I'm a foreigner which for some
Koreans has its own attraction, but that I am
behaving so strangely.

"It's the song," I announced to one of my own
students one evening, who happened to be near the
gate. "Did you hear it'?—immediately embarrassed
that I was so insistent about this business of the

frog. Worse, even, when the frog croaked again, this time loud as a French horn, my student still couldn't hear it. "I can't believe you can't hear it," I said. "No," he assured me, he couldn't. "Christ!" I said more to the frog than to him.

Later in the evening, when it was quiet, I would go out walking, usually to the other side of the campus, along the rice paddies. Few people walk there and in the fall the insects hum like high wire lines and there's a sour stink in the air. Life abounds in this rich Asian mud for which the fast moving swallows are always enthusiastic since they skim off the insects—the topmost layer of Korea's harvest. But by mid-September, when the green rice stalks are three feet high, it's harder to see the long-legged heron unless it's working the edge of the paddy. It moves with the slow deliberation of a surgeon. And it's doubtful that the unsuspecting frog even knows when it's become dinner, the long beak strikes with such precision. It's true, isn't it, we love most what we cannot explain...the death and resurrection of a lumpy world?

The West-Blue Apartments beyond the rice patty are drab on the landscape—concrete poured 20 stories high—except when the sun going down hits the wall of windows, setting the whole building ablaze. But this is the right place to be...the erratic flight of the bat that strains the eyes trying to follow it in last light over the rice fields when it becomes like a small, black glove tossed by a wind. Deep in the field a frog croaks. Nearby a smaller one answers. Two days 'til Chosuk and the moon almost full. The dark of that tea bowl begins to settle in Kwangju.

Kisses

Oh for kisses, portable
and time-honored
and no one country's invention.

Koreans brought theirs
down with them
from Mongolia
on black shaggy horses
years and years ago—
this wet way
all over the world
we have of putting our heads
together, untying with the lips
the words our tongues knot.

Whether it's the oldest kiss
alive, we really don't know,
the one found lying on its side
in sedimentary rock
in what is now Somalia
by a villager herding his white cows.
In geologic time
archaeologists put it somewhere
between the sloth and the musk ox.

Oh for kisses that are never dated,
can't be,
especially the dark, red ones
that like to hide themselves

behind closed, Korean doors
and which, by all accounts
are doubly good
being so indecent.

Love

Is there any consolation in knowing
we are all failures at it
or its derivation, defeat, trying to avoid it?

Maybe you don't want to read this,
so try Puget Sound
in early morning light
when you might catch an eagle
sliding over the wrinkled water—
that's lovely enough
especially with a hot cup of coffee in your hand—
a little respite from love
but like the tide, defeat always returns.

Look at it this way, I'm in love too.
Anything less would be a waste of time.
I include bird-watching, though sighting an eagle
can make one forget, for awhile, his failures—
the hooked beak, yellow eyes.

The first woman I loved killed herself,
although if you had seen her black hair,
heard her laughter,
or the fight she put up to live—
no eagle was more fierce.

I'm not going to lie to you
about love, how it breaks us all in the end
for sure, but usually long before.

Maybe you do what I do,
imagine you are a better person then you are.
The little lies are alright, I think,
to get us from one sunset to the next.
But more and more I hear the water lapping the
shore
and it frightens me, maybe you too,
with its frankness.

The second woman I loved
loved me too, but no one wants to know
how love fails, for no special reason
like random driftwood
or tangled rope
or the odd ketchup bottle,
half empty, coming ashore.

Meditation

All afternoon it snows.
I sip whiskey by the window
and watch the little grove of bare trees
below my apartment grow darker.
What is happening to me
anyway that I feel so alone?
I'm really too old for this
I want to say but know better.
What poet in his right mind
would protest love
and I spell it across the wet surface
of the glass with my finger.
It's the beginning of something
I had better toast
I think and raise my glass to the trees,
to the white sky.
The warm Scotch seems to understand,
first sweet on the lips
then burns all the way down.

Bathhouse

One street light still on.
Not dark not light.
Did I sleep at all?
A dog barks, once, twice
but its heart's not in it.
Snow falls through the yellow glow
like a bowl of white moths.
Below, a door opens,
closes. A woman moves quickly
through the shadows
then disappears around a corner
on her way to the bathhouse.
Mornings are hardest, my love
and now winter,
cold wind blowing the snow
over the sidewalk.

The Bean-Paste River

Love drove us to it
if someone should ask,
in a little white car
with push-button windows
and front wheel drive
that made going
down the dangerous bank
and over the round stones
possible, some spinning out
from under our wheels
as we slowly rolled over them
on our way to The Bean-Paste River.

Where we passed out of Korea
exactly, I don't know,
perhaps where the white egret sailed in
over us, extending its black legs
for a landing. Or when we felt a warm wind
humming in our ears, "Don't hesitate."

What's true is: all philosophy comes down,
finally, to lettuce
being rinsed in river water
and a woman's black hair
falling loose over her shoulders.

All around us insects
whine like high-wire lines
and above them the clouds
reminding me of accumulation,
of moving, once again the furniture.

Oh where are we going anyway
better than this,
our clothes flung on the sun-lit rocks
where we left them going in,
into the bean-paste,
into the Bean-Paste River.

Haydn

It's a sweet secret only I know
and the cello and the snow—
love prefers the quiet street in winter
and it was not different then
when Haydn took his evening walks.
So, when white flakes caught
in his unruly hair as they so often did,
he smiled a little,
took note of the mystery of woman,
thought about the two fingers
of warm whiskey he'd left in his glass
in his drawing room. He could do that,
Haydn could, as easy as falling off a wet
Austrian curb, see in her curved hips
the soft glow of the cello
or in the bow's tension, the legs out turned.
"Its shape is first glimpsed in the ankle,"
he liked to say of writing the concerto.
Before his concert one evening
while dressing, he told his valet
who was, just then, holding up
the maestro's black coat,
brushing it,
that he, the composer
was practically a woman himself.
He didn't elaborate, only walked over
to the window and pointed
outside to the fresh fall of snow
while he carefully wrapped the silk scarf
around his neck.

Sea . . . Garden

The sun going down
in the sea, the oldest garden,
and a wooden boat,
its blue paint faded, half chipped away,
coming in now
rounding the immense stone jetty.

Voices, laughter, engine rumbling, the rope
expertly looped
around dock cleat.
Talk about the catch, where to fish
tomorrow.

Too dark to see now, only the lapping
of water on piles, stones and
is there some place to have in mind
on your body to kiss more, say,
than another when kissing
begins in earnest in all the wet places
dark flowers grow.

The Emptiness of Words

...last visit to Paek Yang Sa

It was easier in the past to be a monk. Fewer people
in the world meant fewer words. But even then,
hundreds of years ago, it was hard to get away from
words. It's no accident that temples were built in
remote places, deep canyons, on cliffs and other
impossible places to reach without a serious effort.
And when words did come they had to walk.
Nothing discourages words like a long walk through
wild country, especially when there are bandits and
tigers to contend with. But not anymore. Now they
come by the millions, riding inside shiny new cars,
large buses, and even in taxi cabs to the temple. They
like to picnic. They like to take each other's picture
with Buddha in the background or they stand in
front of a stupa or on the steps of the temple for
group pictures. But all the time they talk, so many
words, in fact, that they create a din of words, first
swirling around on the ground, then banging into
each other, into the walls, the trunks of trees and the
ancient stupas, thousands of words, but lighter than
air, they rise up, most of them, after a while, over the
heads of the people, over the cars, drifting even
above the black tiles and sway-back gables of the
temple. Some drift up faster like burnt paper,
catching momentarily in the elm tree, the
persimmon. That's the good thing about words—
their emptiness—so like dustballs they float up...and
eventually away. The monks know this. They hide
out in the monks' quarters. Or if the weather is
warm enough, play a private game of badminton.
Either way they wait. Soon a wind will come along

or darkness. What words don't leave on their own—
the ones that get inside the temple—the monks
sweep out later. But sometimes when a monk finds
an interesting word which has settled on a table or
on the dark floor of the temple, he may pick it up
and turn it over in his hands, even show it to
another monk. It is only dangerous if they begin to
talk about it. They know this. For them it is more a
meditation on the emptiness of words. And night,
when it comes, especially on Sunday, is a great relief
to the community. Sometimes a few monks will
gather at the front gate to send off a last visitor.
When the car begins to roll away, leaving them in a
little cloud of words, one or two of the monks will
wave. Maybe they will stand there in the dark for a
full minute, not moving at all, just watching the red
taillights grow smaller.

III

Mantra

No work to do
is how I know I've failed
also

the sun coming up
didn't lay a glove on me.

No blame.

My face in the mirror
where I'm getting back
the bad breath
of a promise to be more.

What defeat
that I can't charm this secretary
also

at the signal
I have to sit in the broken
exhaust of my car.

It's a beginning.
Breathe it in.

B o u n d   A w a y

Nature is not so clever
to have raised us up like birds
in such variety that my friend
thinks my grief is all chestnut
while hers is persimmon.
Still, I love this sadness
our loneliness perfects.
The moon, if we think about it,
is asocial. It prefers the bare tree
to the full one—she in her country,
me in mine, we walk the cutbank
at night, where the river flutters
silver, adjusting its feathers.

Korean Noodle

"The thing about it is,"
he said,
(sucking the long white noodle
up
into his mouth,
at the same time
spinning his index finger
the way my father used to
keeping rhythm
to the music of Clyde McCoy,
while doing the shuffle
in the kitchen,
1945,
my mother beaming,
the end of it
suddenly disappearing
into the little black hole
his lips make),
"eventually we die."

Star L3R-379

Twig fire,
I bend my head
out the window
not for the moon
coming on
all sexy
down the runway
but for you
whose dim light
flickers
from so far away
I lose you
the way I sometimes
lose myself
in a room
full of people
or alone
when it's cold
and I have only
a little wood
to put on.

Unju Sa

Just past the field of green peppers
you begin to see them,
an army of long-faced Buddhas
not much taller than I am
but with a lot less to say
after 1000 years of just standing there,
a stone boat that could not turn itself around.

So they stare out past us at the same landfalls,
witness to the wars fought there,
to the endless generations of Kims and Barks
tethered like their black goats
to the land, to crops that failed, crops that didn't.

Everywhere, behind pine trees,
under rocky cliffs, they lean like old ironing boards
or soldiers, propped up, forgotten so long
and so long in one place
lichen have painted over the mouths,
the head-long ears and whole, dour faces
down to the hems of their stony gowns,
star clusters that glow red and yellow in the rain.
Grandfathered into a canyon so narrow
45 years ago bombs couldn't get in.
What's another war to Buddha—restless men
peeing on their own shoes.

His nose, all that once protruded,
more gnawed down now than the rest of him,
went, long ago for tea—a "little Buddha" steeped,
according to legend, brought women boy babies.

On top of the hill, where the mast might have been,
two immense Buddhas sleep through it all,
nestled in like lovers, perhaps the best answer
stone can give
to the next generation and the next,
to be quiet, to hold each other.

Walt Goes With Me

I fought it the way I fight a cold
coming on.
"I don't need this," I said,
thinking, already, about loss,
the car slamming into him,
the dead dogs I'd already buried.
Let's be frank,
we come to witness what a dog brings:
unexpurgated farts,
puke too good to pass up.

"Throw the ball, Tom," Walt says,
dropping the wet thing on my chest
after pushing his head under the Korea Herald
I'm trying to read.

You may well ask, why the name Walt?
Whitman I'd answer fast for the poet
who wanted to be of use
so nursed the wounded on the Union side,
holding up their heads to drink,
feeding them ice cream he bought
out of his own pocket
and most died anyway.

We come from different stars
he tells me, late one night, with his eyes
peering out through a thicket of black hair
his head resting on my leg.

It's true. His occult poems are written in piss
on tree trunks, curbs, on a single leaf
he strains on his leash to read.
My job: to attend in this world
he shamelessly humps.

Sons

A couple of hanara butts
the Korean laborers across the street
stuck into fresh green turds
one of them shit behind a tree
after the lunch break—their idea
of free speech,
the last dirty joke after watching 100
or so beautiful coeds with book bags
and pretty umbrellas
traipse through the construction site,
the mud on their shiny boots.

What can they do now
but go back to work, the coarse sonnet
of hot-pour cement the red pump truck
boom spews out, 1000 pounds a minute
is what I mean by a weighty poem.

"Come back here Tommy," my father would say
when I didn't meet his standard
of clean up. Then hold up his expensive
enamel trim brush. "That's god-damn paint
in there you haven't cleaned out."
So I know about the shit jobs. Rejection.
The lonely lunch break. "Don't flinch asshole,"
he'd say to Billy, my gentle brother,
who at nine could sketch like Monet,
"I'm not going to hit you."

Oh dear light, kindness, you've come too late.
Most of your sons are broken
before the building ever goes up.

Snow in Kwangju

Down here
we see
what snow becomes
from its slow
sideways
decent
quiet
a white handshake
that promises
not to last
in red earmuffs
and black galoshes
we dress up for it,
take a picture
all of us in it—
Tony, fifty-ish,
handsome
in his winter,
Ellen, gloved hands
packing a snowball.
Me.
Then slush,
the principal argument
dying puts up—to thaw,
to take it all back.

When the Old Man Died

...for David Ignatow

the crackers
in the red
plastic basket
survived
but not the over
turned
bowl
of hot chicken
soup
that spread
out its yellow contents
along the counter
then dripped
over the edge
some of its steamy
white noodles
hanging on.

Rend

1.

So, why couldn't I see
from all the years
of dragging the ground
that one gray eye
had grown so much
lower
than the other.
What passes
for life now
is not only morning
light
etching out the mountain
or that white scarf
of smoke
from the brick chimney
west flowing.

2.

I would have fucked it up,
sent him whatever he wanted,
money, paints.
How many times
have I read the letters
every one of them
and come to love
his unhappiness.

3.

Say storm and mean sea
closing over
whatever argument
the boat tries to make
to move forward
and trailing back
into a vast, gray sky
black smoke
from the two, tall stacks.
Everybody along the railing
scared
they've been painted so small
you can hardly make out
what's really going on.
Just the commotion
in reds and dark browns.
Someone trying to haul down
a lifeboat.

4.

The lighthouse means to fool us
throwing its white voice
out into the dark.
I don't know.
Color has its own logic,
words too, juxtaposed
the wheelhouse
is the last to know
everything below
is under water.

Lucky Star

Isn't it a wonder
the way we sail out every day
under nothing more than our lucky star.
Big waves.
Little waves.
The shriek of birds.
We go where a round world takes us.
The darkside boards glisten
with sea water.
So, tie your hair back
love, the only provision,
like the barrel of salted pork we'll need
and hard, white biscuits.
In these waters, sometimes there's no wind
to blow us home.
C'mon my sweet, everything we need
we came with.
Look how the light loves you
coming in over the oar locks
and spreading out along your forearms—
who has so much strength? Don't say a word.

Ginkgo Tree

The knee-high juvenile smile
in the slender trunk of the little ginkgo tree
planted between the curb and the sidewalk
won't tell you anything
about what happened here
in Kwangju at this intersection a year ago
when our bus smashed into the blue pickup.
It raised up on its right side
the little truck did
almost turning over
then settled back down
in an animal gentleness
in a shower of tempered glass
driverless, the door flung open
going now in a whole new direction
coasting, as it were, toward the little ginkgo tree
rolling ever so slowly
dragging its chrome trim along the street
while one of its silver hubcaps rolled
in the opposite direction,
toward us, pointing an accusing finger, I thought.
But if one discounts the dead driver
lying next to the curb
then the little truck, its black tires
carrying it away down the block
took on a certain charm,
the blue door waving back as it rolled
ever so slowly toward the curb
where it bounced softly like a beach ball

then struck the young tree, not such a hard blow,
but enough to ring all of its bell-shaped, green leaves
causing two or three to fall,
one landing on the hood
the other two on the blue cab.

IV

Bowl

My American pants are hanging over the chair
in the corner with your Korean dress.
Over there they can decide foreign policy.
But here we are like two spoons
you and I
in the same warm bowl,
Buddha's bowl, where we, too
can barely open our eyes
having discovered the sweetness of one tongue,
the curves and folds of the inner walls
we breathe hardly at all.
We're held there in a stillness
like porcelain.
We gaze out the window
and then smile in the dark
at discovering a pair of my shorts
hanging on the line
stirred now and then by a little breeze.

Sun Am Sa

The bread we didn't eat
we rolled into little balls
and fed to the fish in the pond below the temple.
Brown and not pretty at all to look at,
they came out from behind the rocks
in a frenzy that surprised us.

Suddenly your large Asian eyes
filled up with a war 48 years dead
and long before you were born.
"You Americans are so powerful," you say,
more to the fish,
tears rolling over your high cheek bones.

I sit there in the sun
by the pond, looking at my American hands,
then at the temple for some kind of clue,
but there is so little to go on.
GMC comes to mind and AC Spark Plug
in Flint Michigan
along the river where I grew up.
Bill Hourigan's brother—I remember that—
Eddy, he went to Korea. He went through the windshield
of Bill's Ford Coupe two nights after he returned. DOA.
First time I'd heard that expression.

"The old people say the soldiers threw candy
and chewing gum from the tanks."
I look down the road, past the temple,
half expecting a platoon of soldiers.

In Asia, I'm telling you, there is no use for logic,
what made the F-51 the best fighter plane
in the Korean Conflict
is of no interest to Buddha
or the woman beside me
who says she's sorry. I say no, it's OK.
Then we make more dough balls
for the hungry fish.

But I know too, the holy relics of youth
are still a fist my hand wants to make
given to me out of love
when Uncle Burt bought them at the Army Surplus
in Saginaw: a red squadron patch of two fighters
coming out of a white cloud, the ingenious green shovel,
collapsible, like the pup-tent and black compass
that points, unfolded now, to memory
and to the heart which says, "Yes, you've found it,
now dig over here."

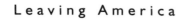

Leaving America

What's left to do,
turn off the lights
lock the door.
This is the way
we say goodbye
to the black Ford.
I know I have loved you
way too much
in this life
sat by you
alone
along the river
when we took my grief
more than once
to the water.
Out of town
time slowed down
to the ticking
of your engine.
I could be so still
down in the grass
black birds
unafraid
walked up the mud bank
only a few feet from us.
I don't know how
to explain my feelings
now
all these years later
getting inside you

(the warm upholstery)
starting you up
when I was so lonely,
rolling the window down.

Oatmeal

...for General MacArthur

There must be enough water in the oatmeal during
the boiling stage to thoroughly cook the raisins.
Otherwise, they will not swell sufficiently to release
their sugar. This is what I would have told the
General. In beginning the moral day, one should try
to remember this. And the process should not be
hurried either by turning up the flame. "You're nuts,"
I can imagine him telling me. Still, I would have
urged him not to hurry his morning, to go to the
window, to watch the morning light spreading out
over the roof tops, in the puddles of water in the
street below. He didn't like windows. Worried about
being a target. When the room fills up with its
frothy odor, you'll know the oatmeal is ready, I'd tell
him. If the General had only tried to understand
this, or had learned better eating habits growing up
in Little Rock, Korea might not be divided today. But
he wasn't a man who could look very deeply into his
porridge. Wasn't able to meet the day on its own
terms which are never negotiable. It seems he only
ate to live and as any Korean will tell you, that's
getting it all backwards. I can see him now, the 'old
man' at his headquarters in Tokyo, sitting alone in
the large dining room, in his white, terrycloth robe,
going through the motions of eating breakfast,
anxious to get into his day, into his newly pressed
blouse with its 5 immense stars waiting for the
Supreme Commander in the other room in the arms
of his personal orderly. His mind is already out on
the runway, though, on the new squadron of B-50s

coming in from Okinawa. He's excited about the capability of these longer-ranged bombers. But this was long ago now...so many dead, including the General, the Peninsula almost 50 years divided. But morning, the moral day, still comes. And in cooking, the laws of natural phenomena continue to prevail over love and war. The oatmeal will not be rushed. Or the raisins will not swell sufficiently, giving us the kindness of their sugar.

"A Buddha's been run over,"
the sad patrolman says, averting his eyes
while assuring us
there are people coming to deal with this,
then he walks back to the next car
to deliver the same terrible message,
his shoulders bent.

We can do nothing
but settle back into our seats
and grow wistful, reflective
about what's up ahead.
It's not that there is glass to clean up
or metal wreckage—that would be easy—
but something else in the road
we would rather not look at.

Outside it is gray, threatening rain.
Rice paddies and coarse winter stubble
surround the lines of cars
that stretch back for a mile.

"The arm of Buddha reaches out to everyone,"
my Korean friend says, grinning from the back seat.
"That's very good," I say, but it's already too late
to stop us—the squeals
of unholy laughter fill up the car.
This is exactly the coarseness we were warned about
as children, that we would grow up
to take nothing serious.

But that's not true now, I'm thinking.
And didn't I say rain earlier, but it's snow
that's beginning to fall
in big white flakes.
When they settle on the warm hood of the car
they melt away, but in fields,
on the road, on the tops of the cars, they begin to stick.
We are quiet for a long time just watching.
When the patrolman walks back by us
it is almost dark.
He pauses in the glow of the red taillights
his warm breath a pink-white cloud
in front of his face, floating up
over his head.
He has snow on his black hair,
on his shoulders.
He points to it and smiles.

In the Temple on Monday the roof is gone,
just a lot of polished shards
scattered around on the steep ground
with no place to park a car.
So when it rains or snows
or the wind blows
it all comes inside. Few people go there.

It's messy, slow going and there's damn little meat
there when you finally get inside the black shell.
Korean crab is small, that's all there is to it, but the
red-pepper soup it's cooked in is like Chinese
malatang. Meaning it burns you both ways and
somehow you're thankful for the pain. I just wanted
to sit there in the sweatlodge of my spiritual soup,
spoon it in, and mostly not talk. Not have to struggle
through another English conversation with Mr. Bark,
the fat banker sitting across from me. So far so good.
He and Mr. Jeong my long-time friend were carrying
on in Korean. Back to money matters, I figured, and
the details of a very big construction loan. That's
what this trip was mostly about, in the car, on the
golf course, and now in the restaurant. I'd come
along because Mr. Jeong invited me. It seemed like a
good idea. A trip to the countryside. A walk around
a private golf course where I mostly held up
everybody's game with my slices and hooks.

We were finishing off the day with a special
dinner of crab soup in a famous restaurant in
Hwasun. Crab soup, according to Korean lore, has
immense restorative power, especially for men, their
virility, if you know what I mean. We have our own
private room. We're seated on the floor, the table
covered with 15 different kinds of panchan—small
dishes of traditional foods: garlic mushrooms, bean
paste and fresh green peppers, wild bracken from the
mountains, stuffed clams, five different kinds of
kimchi and so on. It's a feast. Adjumma's running
back and forth seeing to all our needs. I've just

ordered the third bottle of soju. The booze has taken the tension out of my shoulders, my legs, and I'm sweating pretty good now from the crab soup. We all are. I'm pouring his glass full again when Mr. Bark looks up from his bowl toward me and with that look that means he's going to use his English now. I try to look interested. He's sweating even more than I am, from the red pepper, and struggling with a toothpick to dislodge a piece of crab from his teeth. He said it was crab. There's a neat little pile of dark shells beside his bowl.

"You American lucky...big," he said and winks at me, at the same time pointing down at the table right in front of him.

I spoke too soon. "What d'you mean, big?" I said.

Mr. Jeong, showing the fatigue of the long day and the soju, wears a benign smile on his face. He only nods.

"You are long dicks," Mr. Bark said, milliseconds before I picked up the drift of Mr. Bark's pointing.

"No," I said, "You mean, we Americans have long dicks, (pause) that's probably how we'd say it in English." Then I point down at the table too. Mr. Bark stares where I point. Adjumma pulls back the door and comes in with the traditional finishers, little cold bottles of sweet soy milk. She sits one in front of each of us. He's quiet a little longer while he continues to probe his teeth for the crab. I'm thankful. Mr. Jeong's eyes are glazed over like he's gone back to the double bogey he got on the 17th hole to play it over again. Lots of laughter from a party of men in the next room.

"Chokum!" Mr. Bark says suddenly and holds his index finger and thumb a couple of inches apart over the pile of crab shells to show me. At the same time he makes a sad face and casts his eyes down toward the table, over his crotch. I want to be angry with him, but I'm not. He's just trying to be funny. I wish his dick was bigger but I don't tell him that. I'm thinking about mine, now, down there under the table, bred in America and all of that...the Founding Fathers—their dicks, too, in order to form a more perfect union.

"C'mon, Mr. Bark," I say, "It really doesn't matter." But I can see he doesn't want to hear that lie. He shakes his head. He wants details. He holds his hands apart the way a fisherman will to show the size of the fish he's caught.

"How big yours, Mr. Tom?" he says.

"I understand you, Mr. Bark, but you've got to get your verb in there," I say.

"Bigger, huh, than" and he moves his hands further apart, "this," all the time grinning, his eyes rolling.

"Kapsida!" Mr. Jeong says, "Let's go."

Mr. Bark brings his hands down, knocking the little pile of shells into his lap. He squirms around. I look away, relieved. We struggle to our feet like old men and move toward the doorway where outside we sit down again to put on our shoes. We're all puffing and sweaty and red-faced. Then we pass out of the restaurant, single file, walking on a wet, cement floor, past adjumma who is bowing, past the bubbling tanks of fish, the metal tubs of live crab.

Dogs

I.

Our pals
in the world
they come in more varieties
than fish,
both alive and dead.
We're all being tested
behind the pound in Flint
the homeless
euthanized
and dumped
into 50 gallon drums,
heads, tails, feet
hanging out,
food for flies.
Look at this Tommy,
smell it.
Puking
is a perfect score.

2.

The monk at the door
said, "After you, I'm first,"
and let the dog in.
You might think from this
there is a heaven

of animals
and that would be right,
wouldn't it?
Whatever we can imagine
is plausible.

3.

Let's clear away the confusion,
"stamina food" in Korea means
doing something about the pudding
between the legs
where once there was an erection.
The stone god on its knees
is always an occasion for nervous chuckles
and the ordering of dog soup.
No time to gaze at the constellation Orion.
I tried that—take the long view
with the dog twisting on a rope,
suffocating, unable even to scream
with its jaw tied shut—it doesn't work.
Terror is the white noise of nails
clawing the air, life inched out of the mutt
so slowly the blood is like a hotshot
hauling its freight to all the muscles.
That's the plan. Heaven, overhead,
too big to see
and cold. Morning in the world
cruel, manageable.

4.

Suzy,
25 years later
I follow your cement tracks
across the garage floor
to the place
where I was kneeling
that day
in the hot sun
working the trowel.
Your hard photograph
of paws
is wearing away too
I notice
where they stop
abruptly
where the wall
was later built
below the broken window
of cobwebs,
the soft light
pouring in.

5.

Down the block
a light comes on.
Oh plausible dog
we're scared
of what's out there
with your barking,
trees

clouds
our locked up cars
in the driveways
with frost on the hoods,
little signs stuck in the lawns
in the shape of a badge—
"This Neighborhood
Protected."
We don't dare
turn the light on
inside.
That would give us away
(standing there
alone
in the front room
cold feet
while we peer out
into the dark)
wouldn't it?

The dead eat nothing. The living eat a lot. And now
the dead are beginning to take up too much space on
the Korean Peninsula. At the rate they're going,
according to the living, by the year 2000 they will
have deprived the living of over 100 hectares of
fertile land which might have grown rice or peppers
or even peach trees where the land has a gentle
slope. What to do with them, the deceased, when the
living are torn between their memory and the need
to eat. Burn them, some urge. But to do that kills
them twice over, so the old believe. And it's hard to
fault a belief once it takes root in the mind of the
living. The dead, so far as we know, have no mind
with which to debate this issue, so it's easy to ignore
whatever opinion they might hold. It would be good,
just once, to hear from the dead. They might say,
"For Christ-sakes, burn us and plant peppers and
over there put in a grape arbor." But that would
make the world a sensible place in which to live and
much less interesting. When my American mother
died she said just before, "Tommy, get rid of the
body. I don't need it anymore." She meant it. She
would have been comfortable in Korea as a Buddhist.
Like them, even alive she didn't like the idea of
taking up too much space. Dead I'd still want duk
galbe, but that's just wishful thinking—hot-bone
soup—with a bottle of chung hae. Some mul
kimchi. Personally, I wouldn't want to be a big

enough memory in anybody's head to expect them to put me ahead of a garden—black soil, water, the smell of the earth. What I'm saying is, in life, if I had to choose between memory and strawberries, I'd choose strawberries every time.

Magpie

...Korea's goodluck bird

When the stick lands at my feet
the magpie settles down on the roof
nearby to see, I suppose,
what I'm going to do about it.
It's snowing, after all, and cold February,
so hard, even for a poet
to think of first buds and nest-building.

I would have let the matter go
and gone my human way
if his mate, a slightly smaller,
more determined bird
had not suddenly joined him
on the ledge where together now
they seem to want to force the issue—

Did God create the earth in six days
and rest on the seventh
or didn't he, in which case
the stick would be falling, more accurately
from Heaven, would it not?

But then I have to wonder
why these two over-achievers
were working on Sunday,
in the snow,
or are birds exempt

from His holy covenant?

But then again, it might be
merely a pagan stick
falling happenstance
at my feet.
Either way, I'm left to suppose
while my feet are growing cold
and love is on the wing, on the wing

Prayer

I'm cutting my swallows from black silk,
China's best, Father, so that when flying
they meet with the least amount of resistance
and thank you again for the abundance
of insects over the green rice fields
this evening, the water bumpy with frog eyes
reflecting a pink west-flowing sky.

Now, I'm sewing into the material
my red heart because the dead lately
have been a little noisy in my sleep
and about this prayer, Father,
I don't want any confusion—

I'm mud deep here
in love and would like to stay on
awhile longer at least until I get the sun right,
its light over the rim of this bowl
we all eat from, and watching
while I'm at it, the little spot fires
appearing over the back of my hands—

my age, a quiet invitation

to bird watching
where light around the gray heron,
alone in the water,
dies down, in time, to black
and what the imagination can rescue.

Snow

...for the monk, Sung Chol

Look at us. The strain of citizenship
shows in our faces. We work so hard
trying to be this country or that one.
But even in winter the sun warms us all alike.
If you need a name, better to assume the cover of
snow
which we would never call a foreigner
on any shore when it comes
white, blowing in, so lovely
only to fill up our trees, our wells.
Its only tradition—giving itself entirely away
in the world
and equally, to fence post or roof top
or the long road in.
Snow, like zen, doesn't know it's snow.
The brown-eyed baby likes my green eyes
until you tell it otherwise. The names of things
can kill us down to the last town.
In the down-falling snow, in the slowness of it
there are only answers. They settle quietly, every-
where
on Yu Hyeung Ri. Yokohama. Chicago.

Yu Hyeung Ri

I still hear the grunting pigs
you were feeding in the dark, adjumma,
and I was probably wrong
peering at you bent over them
while you carried on a conversation
a large red bucket dangling from you hand,
but you were beautiful,
old, in your plain clothes,
a white towel wrapped around your head,
talking pig-talk in the dark.

What would the Vatican do
I wonder, with your nomination
from sainthood, if I said,
"This one also has God's ear."

Korea, you old, stone-filled boot,
you intend to break me too, I can tell,
and probably in a village like this
with its narrow alleys that dead-end
at pigsties
where there are no night lights
and getting home
means following the white-washed walls.

Notes

Page 7
pu koo bird — these beautiful birds, with the size and presence of
our stellar jays, inhabit the forests of Korea. They derive their
name from their cry: "pukoooo, pukooo." They're occasionally
seen around the mountain temples, especially in the evening.

Page 15
won — Korean currency

Page 29
Mark 8:24

Page 31
Yong bong dong — a district in north Kwangju, where the Chonnam
National University is located.

Page 33
Chosuk — Korea's Thanksgiving and time of ancestral worship,
linked to fall harvest, gift-giving and good fortune.

Page 34
Inspired in part, after reading Tess Gallagher's, "Portable Kisses."

Page 39
Bean-Paste River —"pet name" name of a Korean river, what love
drives us to.

Page 43
Paek yang Sa — Buddhist temple north and west of Kwangju. Go in
the fall when the leaves are in color and when adjumma is
selling *kokum* — dried persimmon, along the road.

Page 53
"A little Buddha steeped..." — it was not uncommon in the past in
Korea for a young, pregnant mother to chip off a little of
Buddha's nose from the ancient statues then add it to her tea
in the belief that a Buddha would grant her a boy-child.
Nothing in Korea, then and now, bestows powers on adjumma
like giving birth to a boy-child.

Page 57
hanara — Korean for the best of something, excellence.

Page 58
hanbok — traditional Korean dress

Page 70
Sun Am Sa — Korean temple

Page 78-80
malatang — a Chinese soup, called "hotpot." A lethal concoction.
    Delicious. Purported to sweat out bad spirits.
Hwasun — a town and suburb south of Kwangju
soju — Korea's national drink. A grain alcohol one soon acquires a
    taste for since it complements so nicely Korean food. At 30%
    by vol., *soju* gives a whole new meaning to "getting drunk on
    food."
chokum — Korean for little, short, not much.
pan chan — a endless variety of "small dishes" one comes to expect
    with every meal. Another of the endless joys of getting up and
    eating in a food culture.
kimchi — pickled cabbage or other vegetables. Ubiquitous, like
    bean-paste, it's always on the table, and usually several kinds.
kapsida — Korean for "let's go."

Page 85
duk galbe — Korean "bone-soup." Served only in the winter. Very
    hot. Heavenly.
mul kimchi — "water" kimchi. Appears white like flower petals
    under the vinegar and garlic flavored water it's served in. Yet
    scrunchy and tender to the teeth, the tongue.
chung hae — rice wine, what we think of as sake. I've had both,
    Japanese and Korean. No contest. Chung hae is superior.
    Again, like kimchi, there are endless varieties.

Page 89
Sung Chol — a famous Korean Buddhist monk who died in 1997.
    He was fluent in several languages. Revered by his country-
    men for his wisdom, powers of meditation and spiritual
    austerity. He was cremated after he died. From his ashes a
    substantial amount of sarie was recovered—the crystaline
    nuggets Buddhists attribute to one's spiritual attainment.
Yu Hyung Ri — small, mountain village north and east of Kwangju.
adjumma — a married, Korean woman. More, principle transmitter
    of both language and culture to the next generation. There is
    no more compelling word in the Korean language.

TOM CRAWFORD'S three previous collections of poems include *If It Weren't For Trees, China Dancing,* and *Lauds,* which won the Oregon Book Award in 1994. He has been recipient of fellowships form the Oregon Arts Commission and the National Endowment for the Arts and his work has been widely published in journals and anthologies. He has lectured and taught at colleges and universities throughout the western United States, taught three years in the Peoples Republic of China, and five years at Chonnam National University, Kwangju, Korea. He now lives in Portland, Oregon.